Skeleton Songs

Savannah Love

For those of us learning to dance

out of our graves…

Contents

Discovery   7

Letting Go   41

Weeping   67

Rejoicing   99

Discovery

Anointing Oil

You paint my forehead
with sweet scented oil.
A figure shaped like the space
you hold for me
in your secret place.

The aroma of your joy
welcomes me home.
It delivers me to a place
of knowing and being known.

As my skin absorbs the oil
my heart embraces the intimacy
of your hands on my face

tracing an eternal path to grace.

Centrepieces

We have heard of pottery

where a broken vessel is resealed

with golden glue to define

the cracks and crevices with beauty.

Putting the brokenness on display

and identifying with it.

Our God moulds the clay

and marbles it in gold.

The broken pieces are part

of the new masterpiece

but no longer the centrepiece.

We do not find identity

in glittered cracks

but in golden hearts

made whole by our creator.

Redefined and reborn in His strength.

Unyielding

His love for you
crumbles the stones
they have thrown at you.

His love for you
destroys the shame
you have buried yourself in.

His love for you
would lay down
His life for you
over and over again.

His love for you
*is as strong as death
its jealousy unyielding
as the grave.
Song of Songs 8:6*

Skeleton Songs

Skeletons hum lullabies on mossy rocks
for restless reeds and skipping pebbles.
Music gushes down a river bend,
into the hollow ear of a winter's breeze.
The sun embellishes His golden
meadow, wishfully waiting
for His skeleton's song.

He imagines a sweet tune,
the kind that breaks a heart
then melts it back together.
A melody of peace
built from broken pieces.

The sun coats his dry bones
ready to soak his sweet, sombre song
and carry His skeleton home.

Knowns and Unknowns

He poured the sacrifice
of His highest vulnerability
for a piece of ours.

Knowing he would face rejection.

We have the luxury of trusting
that our vulnerability in Him
will never be abandoned.

It will be nourished in the blood
that pours from the cross,
down the hill,
and into the temple
nestled in our hearts.

The one He has chosen as home.

Delicate Tides

In the tumble of the seas
the waves crash me
into you.

You carry me through the current.

The turbulence shakes away
everything I thought I knew,
then shows me everything
buried and felt.

An empty home,
hoarded lies,
withered snakeskins,
and a longing
for my abandoned father.

Incense

The incense blankets
the room and your breath
carries goodness.

How sweet is the sound
of your song
on our hearts?

Even the rocks
will sing of your goodness
when the earth grows quiet.

The Span of Eternity

Such fierce and unbounding grace

that has chosen to interlace

us into your eternity.

A masterpiece so expansive

that it stretches the strains of time.

A picture so rich and wide

that it carries

everything my words cannot.

Even so…

It is our existence that you have sewn

into your everlasting tapestry.

Tsunamis

Breathing fire from the ocean belly,
the moon cascaded the tide.

Pearly sand beads danced
in quivering rhythm
with the tremolo,
while the sun cowered
in the depths of the earth

A tsunami of living water
ripped me from the ground
and yet,

I have never been more stable.

Open My Eyes

Let me see a speck of dust
as a building block
you placed in the air.

Let me see the mustard seeds
you faithfully planted
as budding images
of your being.

Let me see them
roaming the heavens
hand in hand with the one
who carried the nails, the keys,
and the heart of the earth.

Heavy Stones

You pulled me out
from under a stone,
reaching into a dark,
haunted crevice.

The kind only you can see.

Even in the loneliest
depths of the unknown,
the warmth of your hands
light the way.

Letters from Heaven

Let the reflection of my face

light up your eyes

so your heart

may see me.

Clothe yourself in the warmth

of my embrace,

so your heart

may feel me.

Hold my hand in the dark place

when your soul trembles,

so your heart

may trust me.

Part your lips to whisper

my writing's trace,

so your heart

may hear me.

Cleanse in my sea of grace

every menacing crevice,

so your heart

may know me.

Be still, and know that I am God.
Psalms 46:10

Moon Dances

Moon dances stir songs

in our souls.

Inescapable melodies

that teach us

to walk in valleys

and light candles

in our shadowed spaces.

The fragrance of our flames

outshines the stars

and pleases the moon.

For she was created

to feel the power

of little night lights.

She knows the son

who tends to them

with the light of eternity.

He Sees You

I have seen my God
grow fruit in the dark places.

I have seen Him soothe
the cry of an adulteress.

I have seen Him raise
eternal life from cruel death.

I have seen Him build
a holy city from exiled people.

I see Him still,
loving His children
from one end of eternity
to the other.

Unspoken Word

Without a word,
you spoke.

My wayward soul
swallowed the sound.

The breath of life
burrowed inside my lungs
and moved my heart to weeping.

You crafted an entire universe,
radiant and expansive.

Yet, the love you poured
into it sits humbly
at the foot of the cross.

Where you reached out your hand
and welcomed me home.

Meeting Place

Thank you, God
for meeting me on this page.

The words you breathe from this ink
bring me into your embrace.

How splendid it is
that my eyes are yet
to meet your face,
but this pen can trace it
through any moment.

You meet me here.
Every. Single. Time.

Life Blood

God's goodness transforms scars
into stories and victories.

Broken pieces become tapestries,
whispered words become prayers,
silent tears become wells
of anointing oil.

The blood of Jesus cultivates life
in the desolate place.

I Am Yours

Mountains quiver
at the sound of your name.

Mighty life-giving power
radiates the span of existence.

The vibration of your glory
moves the dry bones into dancing.

The grave loses its grip
on all you have made yours.

Keys

His final breath slipped

from His lips

and crushed the temple.

They say endings

create new beginnings

but not many know

of the continuations

in between.

The wounds that bled

on that night will be carried

 in His hands for eternity.

Still, He holds the keys

claimed in the in-between.

Brittle Bones

Gushing and tearing,

these waters pull apart

my bones.

Even so, they float…

dry. brittle. broken.

How long before I can taste

the wine from these waters?

Does hope really look like this?

Can restoration

be built from brittle bones?

Quenching is formed
from the tides of time.

Eternal life was dug out
from the most harrowing grave.

Life in Jesus is birthed
from the death
of our flesh.

Brittle bones make way for the king
who transforms them into new life.

Into Your Hands

The incense of His tears
pooled with the power
of His blood.

When His final breath fell,
the temple collapsed with it.

The weight of death
was released
as life.

'Father, into your hands,
I commit my spirit' Luke 23:46

Lavender

Lavender-laced gravestones
beckoned my shattered soul
to rest.

They promised to drain
my strength and release
me from living.

But, as I buried
my knees in the soil
I came face to face
with He who is life.

His hand held mine
and pulled me
to His cross.

It was here

that He claimed
these graves and gifted
the joy in mourning.

He brought freedom
out of sacrifice.

Backbones Crack

Backbones crack,
as my spine slides
under the weight of grace.

All the things we should have carried
feel like a breath
compared to the ferocious,
steadfast mercy
of our father.

My bloodstained hands
can't hold everything
the Lord has poured
into my salvation.

But, with weak knees
and a melted heart,
I kneel before the throne.

Blanketed in the palms
of the one who chose
to hold me.

Giants

Giants quiver at the sound of laughter.
They tremble knowing the strength
of His blood on our hearts.

Jesus climbed the cross
to meet their eyes.
They saw the victory
nailed in His hands:

our victory
over them.

So when they beckon
the worries of your heart
strike them with life's sting
for He has conquered death.

All I Have

Weariness seals the eyes of my heart.
Rain thundering in my skin,
soul tossed around in the flood.

"Adonai, why do you
leave me to drown?"

The living water filling my lungs
seems to suffocate my strength.

Thunder electrifies my heart,
she quakes in your presence.

You throw me into the storm
promising that one day,
I will understand your goodness.

Your promise is all I have.

Life Proceedings

You carry me to the desolate place
where we mourn the death of my heart.
Fragments of things held captive
lie abandoned in sand.

We bury the broken bones
in the depths where they are claimed.

Some sad stories have happy endings
and some deaths have new beginnings.

The one who raises the dead
is the one who raises me.
The one who presses
new wine from water
is the one who builds
victory from surrender.

On this day, we rejoice
in the passing of me
and cherish new beginnings
planted in my heart.

This heart that rests
in your secret place
and is the most alive
it could ever be.

Letting Go

Oceans

43

Be baptised daily in His intimacy.
Allow living waters to soak
through the garments you
have clothed your heart in.

As you lie in the ocean
of His fierce vastness feel
the weight of where
He has placed you.

Know that when the tide
tumbles your soul
you can breathe Him in.

Submerge

Moonlit waves swirl
with the stars,
pulling my soul
into the depths
of its grave.

Submerged,
you tumble my being
through the current,
leaving me to drown
in the crashes of your mercy.

My heart meets you
face to face
melting at
the sight of your grace.

This tumultuous love
is too much to carry.
More than my shoulders
are worth bearing.

So I baptise it in the sea
where we bury me,

and arise with the strength
to carry you in my heart.

Find Me

Find stillness in your heart

like the waters that reflect

His painted sky.

For in your humility,

your quiet,

your secret place,

His heart will meet yours

and you will see His image

interlaced with your everyday.

Written on My Heart

The new wine stung

my throat as it melted

the debris of everything past.

The salt of the earth

sizzled on my wounds.

The pain He braced

so I could even stand

in these moments

anoints my tears

and humbles my fury.

He is written in hurt

written in suffering

written in death

But He is the author of life.

Vulnerable Offerings

Come as you are
as an offering to me
so I may know
each part of you
intimately.

Share with me the vulnerability
of your heart as a service
for my own heart.

For I have made a place
for you to dwell
in your entirety,
and learn my heart for you.

Hiding Place

I lie hidden

in your secret place,

praying you don't find me.

What will happen when you see

these tear-stained cheeks

and dirty fingertips?

You sing to me

of cleansing blood

but my heart still shakes

at the sight of the cross.

I feel the weight

of the hammer

in my hands.

I nailed your feet

but then,

you washed mine.

Spine Tingles

The weight of the world
cracked my spine.

In the crevice
of the breakage
was tucked
a handwritten letter.

A sweet reminder
that it would get better.

New spaces formed
in intimate places.

Anointing oil spilled
from the spring
of a fiercely gentle healing.

Lighthouse

Jonah wept into the waters.

A roaring reflection

of everything he abandoned.

'Cast me away!' he screamed.

'Let the tide swallow me

so you may be cleansed

of my presence.'

But, in the ocean's death bed

he was carried

      and redeemed

           and redirected.

Autonomy

I will never be enough.
My blood will never cover me.
The stains on my hands
will always cry louder.
The fruit from my striving
will always be bitter.

But you see all of it.
You watch me pace
back and forth
between
death and life.

You wait patiently
for a whole heart surrender
that may never come.

I'm still digesting
the fruit of autonomy.

Even so, you admire
the eclectic pieces created
in this mess and smile.

It's everything and nothing
like you hoped.

The Carrying

Sacrifice the need

to carry your burden.

Leave room

on your shoulders

for your cross

and carry it

to the mountain.

As His blood is poured

on the altar, rest

your heart at His feet

and wash them in your tears.

Deep Sea

Angels of the deep sea
beckon me from the shore.
The night sky is bright
in my eyes
but the black pool
of living water
is brighter for my soul.

The salt stings and cleanses
the wounds on my feet.
Goosebumps on my legs
remind me of your presence.

The cold water covers my head.
My vision is painted black.

Here in the cooling darkness,
I have never seen you clearer.

Chasing

Chasing after the wind
is the torture of losing myself.

Searching the depths of my soul
for the things that lie above me
and digging the heels of my heart
to hide from things hung on His cross.

Vapour

Vapour in my lungs.
Vapour dripping from the sun.

Vapour in the air.
Vapour in things not there.

Vapour is a familiar sound.
Vapour sends me spiralling around.

Vapour was birthed from your breath.
Vapour falls in the face of death.

Unborn Repentance

Father, I am tired.

My body ceased
to carry your strength
when I let go
and pulled out my own.

White-knuckled fingers
won't let go.

I hold myself hostage
in this self-built bomb shelter.

I need you,
even when I can't say it.

please,
don't let go…

Defrosting Keys

Gentle cracks of weathered lips
caressed the lies of welcomed spring.
Haunted by snow snaking
through sickened valves; life shivered
when I cast you out.
The ice-sealed door wouldn't budge.
All this anointed oil and still,
I was constrained. frozen. stuck.

The keys melted away with flaking truths
and my eyes refused to leave the ground.
I disjoined love from its source, trampling
the fireplace as my spirit sizzled
in the cinders. What warmth
did I expect to find in a cold hard heart
broken from my mind-made avalanche?

Inhalation stings

and exhalation is the same old thing.

The rubble glares into my soul,

spitting questions, I can't carry.

"How dare you sit with the emptiness!"

Bones fractured in its tone,

"You don't belong here".

Carrying Life

A burial clothed in peace,

the prince knew the strength

He could carry.

He also felt

the fear that we carry.

His hands hold the wounds

of pain

       rejection   falsehood

injustice   evil

    cruelty

SIN.

But His scars

are strong enough

to carry the keys of Hades.

The lamb didn't stay buried

and neither should you.

Cleansing Tide

Even in a breath,

you move the mountains

and cleanse them in the sea.

As I struggle against the current

I cleave to the promise

that you won't leave

my soul to drown.

Though the tumultuous tide

of grace tosses me outside myself,

your cross remains extended.

A lifeboat to carry me

in this infinite pool

of living water.

Mountain Redemptions

The mountain stands tall
in the heart of the sea
that swallowed Him whole.

He knows the God who moves him
and feels the life he planted
from the deepest graves.

He continues to stand
with the vibrations
of oppression threatening
to escape their chains.

He knows the strength
of eternal freedom and the purity
of the blood that fights for him.

Even in the heart of the sea.

At the Well

The weight of emptiness

burdens my heart.

My hands bleeding

from cleaving

to all these broken pieces.

I peer into the well,

mustering the strength

to pull from its waters.

Every single day,

I stand here alone waiting

to be restored. But, still

the emptiness gets heavier…

Here you are,

standing by the broken well.

You remove the shards

from my palms

and wash them

in living water.

Your fullness

is weightless.

In you,

I have the strength

to never thirst again.

Weeping

Ancient Poetry

My God, my God, why have you
forsaken me? Psalms 22:1

These words pooled
and glistened in crimson tears.

His final breath was ancient poetry
written from the heart of a broken father
cleaving to a promise.

My God, my God, why is it so heavy?

The lips that spoke these words
blew down the temple
in the same breath
that they whispered my name.

My God, my God,
you will never forsake me.

Seated in Writings

Here you are,

seated in the writings.

Heavy words spilled

from your lips,

spilled into my soul

and sprawled

onto a page.

Slowly,

I am learning

to trace the world

you breathed into being.

Desert Pieces

Broken pieces

slip through my fingers.

My hollow heart couldn't survive

the desert or even face the sea.

But you walked across the waters.

You fed my soul and recovered

it from the barren place.

My soul thirsts for you Lord,

Psalms 63:1 ESV

Your waters give me life.

Daggers

Daggers of cruelty
shoot from my soul.
Form from the shards
of a broken heart.
These words of mine
tear everything apart.

Unable to reign them in
from my lips,
or set them free
from my mind.

How did it come to this?

Soul struck down
by unforgiveness,
scrambling for life.

If only I looked to you instead.

Buried Beads

Sandstorms tear the world
choking all that is precious.
I am buried in sunburnt beads;
not an olive branch in sight.
As the sun peels my skin
I remember He who kneels above it.
The one who will send His son again
to pave the sand away.

I will dig and trudge even when
it seems the world won't budge
because you built hope
into these sand beads.

I will forage with blistered fingers
until I find it. In your hands,
it is always, always there.

Counting Tears

Catch my tears in a jar

and place them on a mantle.

Press them until they are pure,

pour them into new wineskins.

Let my cries honour you

the way my praises do

as they softly sing from my cheeks

and find their place in your heart.

My own heart will soften knowing

you turn old waters into new wine

and weary hearts into new wineskins.

Broken Stones

The stillness is turbulent.
These buried thoughts
gush to the surface
as the raging hand
of my soul strikes the rock.

Suddenly there is a flood
that I begged for
but can't contain.

Drenched in bitterness
I look toward the promised land.

The distance between where I am
and where you call me
is earth-shatteringly heavy.

The beauty of your heart
is in the way you
graciously meet me here.

Stormy Weather

The storm is a song:
turbulent and wild.

Her light strikes my soul
and brings it to weeping.

The wounds complete
your work within me.

Thunder vibrations dance
beneath my feet.
Her rhythm pushes
the beat of my heart.

The roar of a storm is dark

boisterous

joyful

sharp

dynamic

but most of all…

anointed under the fingertips

that pressed life from lifeless stone.

Ashes

Fear is a tsunami
uprooting my being.
The debris from its waves
haunt me.

My heart is a forest fire
peeling and melting
piece by piece.
The ash is a deathbed
beckoning my weary soul.

But He —
makes my burden light.

And He —
makes my yolk easy.

In Him —
I will be made whole again.

Fingerprints

He carried me
with the holes in His hands
and looked to the centre of my soul.

He wore the scars of His murder
and cleansed the wounds
with His tears.

He saw my fingerprints
on the blade and yet,

He placed my hand in His,
walked me to the throne room
and begged for my salvation.

Unbinding

Sometimes,

you are hard to find.

When my eyes are crowded with tears

and my hands can only feel the ground.

In this mess that swallows my soul,

I can't always find you.

But you,

have found me,

and loved me.

I know you will heal

the blind man within me

so my heart may see your face.

Weeping Stones

When the songs
in our hearts grow silent
and our voices run
dry and barren

the stones in our soul
cry out to Him.

They shout from the remnant
of His promise.

Even when our flesh
crawls and quivers.
Skin scraping on grave gravel
hiding from the heavens;

He hears the tears of our souls.

He nurtures our lament
and turns His ear toward us.

Moonlight Sorrow

Words collide
in a pool of unknowns.
They form from the exhale
of a quiet cry.

The moon covered the sun
and left me in darkness.

This picture of the in-between
squeezed the breath
out of my lungs.

Only the light of the world
could claim life
from here.

Father

Some fathers fall flat
from Earth.
Feet too fickle
to feel the ground.

Some Fathers
lose hold of the son
that burned so brightly
their bones shivered.

Some fathers do stay,
like a hollow carcass
too brittle to carry themselves.
Threatening to break
under the weight
of existence.

When we whisper 'our father'
the one who lives in Heaven…

Sometimes,
our hearts can't find Him.

That word cast out
by every man that ran out.

Even the most loving fathers
carve holes into their children.

Life eternal is found
in a heavenly father
who bleeds love eternal.

Even with holes in His hands
He catches each of our tears
and holds us close to Him.

Flood

I see you in raindrops that crash
and glide on my window.

In brown snakes slithering
from their river beds
and swallowing the light.

In my firewood home
that slips and cracks
under the heat
of these waves.

Grief before resurrection,
crucifixion before redemption.

Sometimes baptism tears
out our insides.

But I see you…

You are the new mercies
that transform
my debris and broken pieces.

Depths and Tides

*Deep calls to deep in the roar of your
waterfalls. All your waves and breakers
have swept over me. Psalms 42:7*

The sorrows of this hour are cleansed
in the hope of tomorrow.
As rain droplets run down my cheeks
I weep with joy knowing

that here as well,
my soul is well
for you spoke at the well.

My tears will water
the seeds you
have planted
for I know you
have anointed them.

Still, you see me

Breathing with my eyes open,
I see towers crumbling
to dust.

I feel the debris strangling
my lungs.

I hear the echoing
cry of Abel.

I smell the odour radiating
from forgotten souls.

I cleave to pieces of things
once known.

I breathe with my eyes open,
because you are watching over us.
Your heart weeping with mine.

Hurricane

My tears are a body of water.
Agitated springs creeping
from the crevices I tucked them into.
They break free and burst
into a hurricane.

As you brush your fingers
through the winds and waters
of these tears, you smile.

Because finally—
the goodness you planted
within me gets to taste
the sweetness of rain.

Pretty Things

I searched for you
in pretty things
but you found me
in rubble and dust.

I struggled to reach you
but you met me here in the depths
you died to save me from.

Over and over again
I cleaved to the glow
of darkness.

But every eternal day
you buried yourself
in my grave
and carried me home.

Graves into Gardens

Your beauty blossoms
in suffering's soil.

In this desolate place
she flourishes,

beckoning the orchids
to grow with her.

She finds warmth
in the heat of destruction.

Her beaming smile radiates
like the Son.

She laughs at the time to come.
Proverbs 31:25 ESV

Pressing

Thank you for the pressing of my heart

and for the tears pouring from my soul.

As you make my heart yours,

I pray this oil will learn

to be refined, purified

and anointed

for your

people.

Amen.

Stitches and Lies

Father, I'm sorry
for worshipping lies
spat in your name.

For cleaving
to each of their words
instead of your own.

I buried myself
in false prophecy
and hid myself
from the truth:

that you,

King of Kings
Creator of the entire universe
made the ultimate sacrifice
so we may taste true life.

The blood of the lamb
speaks declaration
over every single person.

Louder than the lies
I have carried.

Weeping Songs

Music weeps from the olive press as
purity and softness sing from sorrow.

When the sadness trickles
to His feet, leave it free to seep.

Your tears are incense
in its purest form.

Baptisms

Be baptised in your tears

as your heart is made clean

in your repenting vulnerability.

His tears of joy

will be an anointing

on the crown of your soul.

May He wash away any

debris or accusation,

cleansing you for the courts

of your heavenly home.

Lamp Post

Under the glow of a lamp post
you found me shivering.

Everything established
gave light, but the quiet
under the glow was cold.

The shadow stared me down,
threatening to bury me
in the dark wood beyond.

But you soothe me and whisper,
'Every light carries a shadow
but the Son carries life
and the light points to Him'.

All the shadows combined
can't outshine Him.

Rejoicing

Welcome

I crawl into the throne room
carrying everything I have left.

My striving gave little to spare.

The dusty, mouldy pieces
look foreign on the marble floor.
But you say
they are welcome here.

I am welcome here.

Today, I finally accept
your hand. In my heart,
I welcome you here.

Stream of Consciousness

He pulls me into a stream
where my consciousness
weaves and floats.

Letters and whispers flow
from the crevices of my heart
into the written abyss
of everything secretly known.

That's where I find poetry.

Earthly Tongues

You have a secret language written
in the roots of these trees
that only a burial
can decipher.

A poem at sunset
that only the eyes
of a soft heart
can read.

A whisper in the breeze
that only our spirits
can hear.

You speak to us in landscapes
and write to us in birdsongs.
You planted our hearts as trees
so we would know,
we were meant to be.

Weight of Heaven

Find rest in feeling the weight
of Heaven on your heart.

Hold her might and her peace.
Carry the purity of her legacy.

Salvation is heavy
but the emptiness is heavier.

One step at a time, walk with Him.
Cross pressing on your shoulders,
tracing a line in the sand behind you.

He will show you the shelter in sacrifice.

Temple Dust

The oil dripped from His robe
and coated the dust.
The ground was anointed to carry you
and you were called to hold His temple.

Where in your heart will you store Him?
On the throne of the mountains
for all to see?

In the light where He can feel
the warmth of His creation?

Or will you bury Him in the place
he delivered you from?

Blankets

I will not bury the breath

you have poured

into my being.

I will blanket the heavens

in the incense

of my love for you.

For how sweet is the fragrance

of your presence

that it should ever be left

to linger in loneliness.

Scars

Thank you for carrying

the scars of sin in your hands.

When I carry my own wounds

I can see you in them.

I can feel the blood

that covers these hands,

this heart,

and the blade

that made them bleed.

Fields

Fields of evergreen

embrace this place

and your love

covers the roots

of all things.

The tears of joy

from your child who

calls you father.

The tears of sorrow

from your daughter who

doesn't know who she is in you.

The tears of shame

from your son who

can't carry His strength

because he hasn't found yours.

The waters that flow
from your fiercely
loving heart foster life
in the driest fields.

You plant restoration
in the barren lands.

Seat Me with My Enemies

I will find rest in the valley of death

for He has prepared a table for me.

We will feast on His goodness

and break the bread.

When we drink the wine

pressed in the vines

that intertwine His kingdom,

we will do it in remembrance of Him.

Earthquake

My mind is pounding

to the sound of an earthquake.

The ground quivers ferociously

and my bones quake in a brittle rhythm.

The enemy strains with everything

inside himself. Breaking

the earth he fell to

and swallowing

our people from the deep.

Our father pulls us up

through tears and blood

into the light.

One set

      of hands

and feet

      at a time.

Poiema

We are His poetry.
Painted and scribed
by the majestic hands
that sculpted the Earth.

He is an artist breathing life
into forms embellished with grace.
His self-portrait roaming
love-pressed clay.

Words spilling from lips,
speaking life from soil to sky.
His workmanship tending
their carefully crafted gift.

What wondrous love is this?
That He poured His heart
into our existence,
and sealed it with the sacrifice
of His only son…

They are the 99

The Lord is my shepherd:
I shall not want. Psalms 23:1 ESV

These still waters restore

the tears of my soul

as green pastures soften

my heart.

He invites me to feast

with my foes.

In the intimacy of Jesus

I can see Him,

rested in the eyes

of my enemy.

In Him, all is well.

In Him, all are welcome.

Black Ribbon

Ribbons of death tangled
themselves like a vine
strangling a tree.

The pearlescent fruit
stung my lips
and squeezed my lungs.

Sin's banquet is bitterly alluring.
It cloaks itself in false beauties.

There are days
where you will taste and see
the bitter worldly cup.
Remember that feeling!

When you see them at the banquet
don't allow the chains of your own
shame and self-righteousness
to hold them there.

Tapestries

What the Lord has put together
let no man separate.

What the Lord has released
let no man bind.

Nothing can stand in the way
of what God has written
on His creation.

The very dust on our feet
has been placed in our path
to be carried.

He has breathed His life into us.
Let our exhales release
His heart over Earth.

Gethsemane

In the garden,

you carried the weight

of the whole world.

Blood wept

from your hands

as you humbly faced

the devil with love.

My friend, thank you.

For the life

you have given

to live within me.

Willow

Weeping willows lament upstream.

Luscious leaves drip

tears into a grumbling creek.

The ground gasps for air,

grave granules hungry for death.

Even in the most beautiful places

darkness can take the throne.

A soul its footstool.

Even still,

seeds can be planted

with wildflowers.

The tree of life breathing

into ground and sky.

Even here,

He will wrestle the strongman

and reclaim the throne.

Life Works

I have seen you
build a shelter
from an emptied tomb.

I felt my bones quake
when you restored them
out of the grave.

Your creation breathes life.

I can only pray,
that mine breathes you.

Calloused Hands

The callouses on your hands
carry the legacy of His love.

Carry your cross
with the strength of He
who died on it.

Carry the weight
of your people for they
are His children.

Carry each other's burdens,
and in this way you will fulfill
the law of Christ. Galatians 6:2

Seafoam Skies

Seafoam skies open my eyes
to the wonder of being alive.

The hands that paint these clouds
and thread the universe
have clothed me in purpose
and are drawing my path.

He feels the weight
of my sorrows and refines
them into pearls.
He directs light into valleys
and peace into ferocious oceans.

He knows the plans He has for me.

Through life and death
I can dwell in the one
who carries both.

Tender

Sprawled across the floor
lay my dried rose petals,
crinkled and frail
from clenching fists.

We enjoyed their beauty
and bathed in their fragrance.

But today, we carry their mortality.

Beauty is fleeting
charm is deceptive

but a God who stands
tall and tender
through the tides of time,
unshaken by the earthquake…

He is life.

Seashore

Your ethereal peace washes over me,
a flood of new beginnings.
All the pieces of my being
tumble in its tide.

A wave of discovery,
constantly flowing.

You embellish my book
with wholehearted unknowns.

Your grace garnishes
my jagged edges
like sea shells
on a weaving shore.

You complete the sea
and allow its salt
to nourish and cleanse
your work within me.

Wind

The wind carries every fickle thing
that has landed on my cheek.

When I drowned them in my tears,
they flew away.

But you caught them…
You counted their droplets
one

        by

                one

and gently,
placed them in your book.

You have found treasure
in my broken pieces,
hope in my despair,
and a future in my shadowed past.

Skeleton Home

The meadow is lush.

My toes wriggle in the grass,

absorbing the sensation

of new, life-breathed skin.

The sunshine caresses

my goosebumps

and kisses them

good morning.

My dry bones find shelter,

blanketed in the pieces

you built me from.

Now that you have restored me.
My body is learning to dance again.

When you carried me here
in your palms, I knew…

That you built my life
here in this meadow
where dry bones dance
to their new skeleton songs.

Acknowledgments

I would like to acknowledge my wonderful
God who places these words on my heart
and my darling husband Abraham who reads
every one of them!

Thank you as well, Samantha Cabrera and
Erin Samples, for publishing 'Skeleton
Songs' and 'Life Proceedings' in their
online literary journal *Calla Press*.

Calla Press glorifies God in the most
breath-taking way, and it was an honour to
share a small part in their story. Read their
work at callapress.com

I would love to thank you, the reader,
for sharing this book with me.
It is such a blessing that you are here.

About the Author

Savannah Love is an Australian poet who finds God in art and language.

She prays that her writing reveals God's beauty and truth but most importantly, makes room for the all the beautiful things He has to say.

savannahlovewrites.com
savannahlove.writes@gmail.com
@savannahl.writes